United States
Department of
Agriculture

Forest Service

Southern
Research Station

Resource Bulletin
SRS–160

East Texas Harvest and Utilization Study, 2008

Rhonda M. Mathison,
James W. Bentley, and
Tony G. Johnson

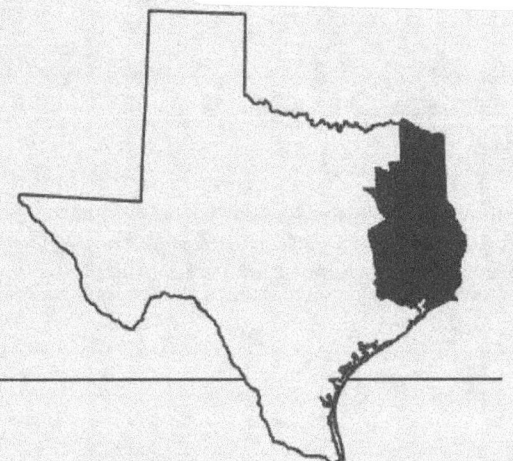

The Authors:

Rhonda M. Mathison, Forester; **James W. Bentley**, Resource
Forester; and **Tony G. Johnson**, Resource Analyst, U.S. Forest
Service, Southern Research Station, Knoxville, TN 37919

July 2009

Southern Research Station
200 W.T. Weaver Blvd.
Asheville, NC 28804

Foreword

This resource bulletin describes the principal findings of a harvest and utilization study conducted during the eighth inventory of eastern Texas' forest resources. Survey crews sampled and measured trees harvested in a variety of logging operations, and analysts calculated wood volume and percent of wood utilization. Harvest volume data and factors for growing-stock and nongrowing-stock logging residue are described and interpreted.

Annual surveys of America's forest resources are mandated by the Forest and Rangeland Act of 1978. Surveys and utilization studies are part of a continuing, nationwide undertaking by regional experiment stations of the Forest Service, U.S. Department of Agriculture. Inventories and utilization studies of the 13 Southern States (Alabama, Arkansas, Florida, Georgia, Kentucky, Louisiana, Mississippi, North Carolina, Oklahoma, South Carolina, Tennessee, Texas, and Virginia) and the Commonwealth of Puerto Rico are conducted by the Southern Research Station, Forest Inventory and Analysis (FIA) Research Work Unit. Unit headquarters is in Knoxville, TN, and FIA has operational offices in Asheville, NC, and Starkville, MS. The primary objective of these appraisals is to develop and maintain resource information needed to formulate sound forest policies and programs. More information about Forest

Service resource inventories is available in "The Enhanced Forest Inventory and Analysis Program—National Sampling Design and Estimation Procedures" (Bechtold and Patterson 2005).

Tabular data included in FIA resource bulletins present a comprehensive array of forest resource statistics, but additional information is available to those who require more specific information. Access to data for the Southern States can be found at: http://srsfia2.fs.fed.us/data/index.shtml.

Acknowledgments

The authors thank Curtis Vanderschaaf and Chris Brown for their review and comments; Anne Jenkins, Carolyn Steppleton, Janet Griffin, and Sharon Johnson for the map, tables, graphs, and statistical checking; and the Southern Research Station (SRS) Technical Publications Team for editorial review, styling, and publication of this report.

The SRS gratefully acknowledges the cooperation and assistance of the Texas Forest Service in collecting harvest and utilization data. Appreciation is also extended to forest industry and loggers for allowing access to their land and logging operations.

Contents

[a]All tables in this report are available in Microsoft® Excel workbook files. Upon request, these files will be supplied in the format the customer requests.

The use of trade or firm names in this publication is for reader information and does not imply endorsement by the U.S. Department of Agriculture of any product or service.

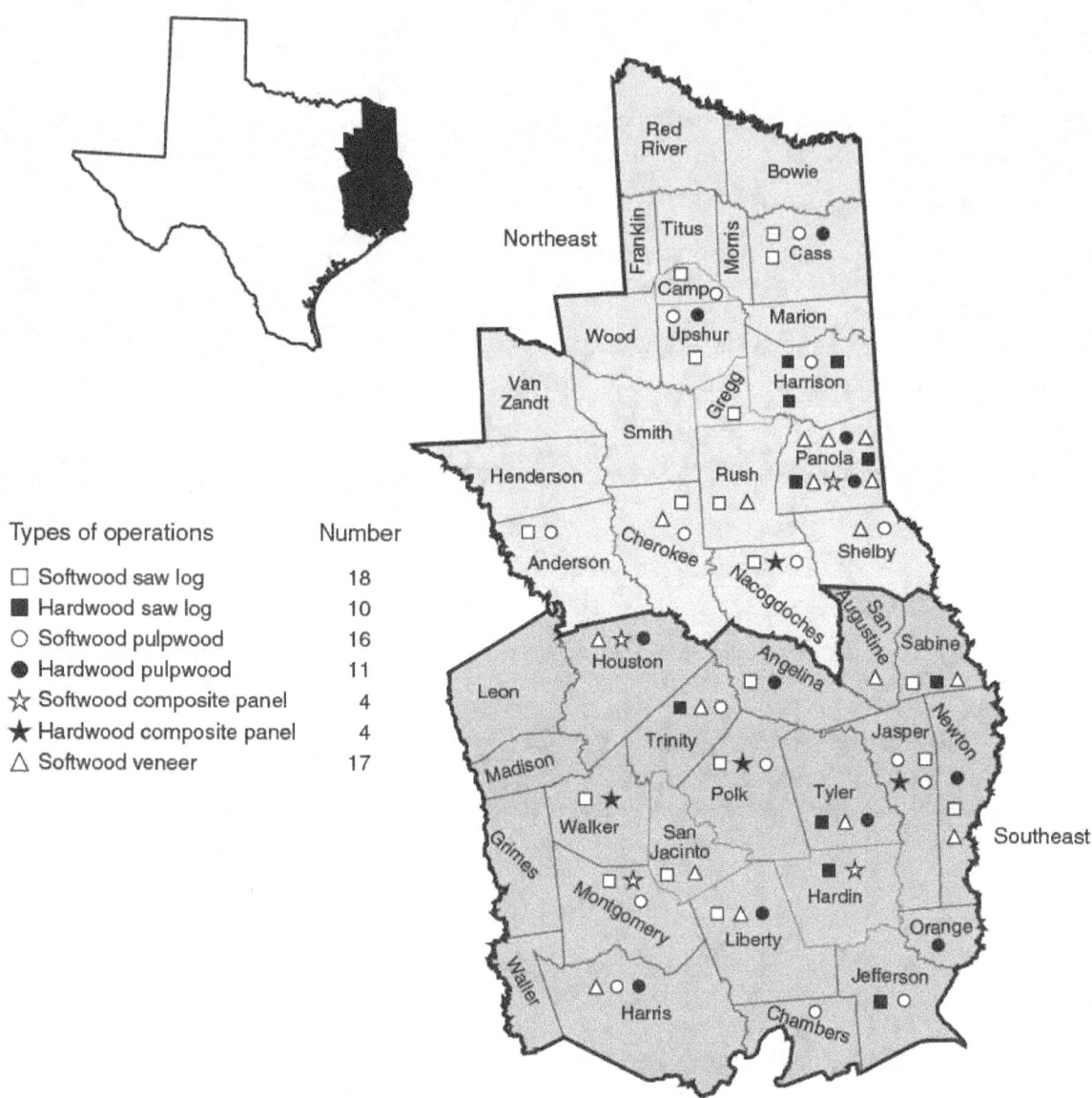

Types of operations	Number
□ Softwood saw log	18
■ Hardwood saw log	10
○ Softwood pulpwood	16
● Hardwood pulpwood	11
☆ Softwood composite panel	4
★ Hardwood composite panel	4
△ Softwood veneer	17

Figure 1—Harvest operations, east Texas, 2008.

East Texas Harvest and Utilization Study, 2008

Rhonda M. Mathison, James W. Bentley, and Tony G. Johnson

Introduction

Forest planners and managers have a continuing need for information about the timber resource, and the general public is expressing increasing interest in the effects of logging. Therefore, up-to-date data on the Nation's forests—and how they are changing—are essential to well-informed decisionmaking. Information about the condition of and changes in the timber resource of Texas comes from three primary sources: (1) inventory plots, which describe current conditions and quantify changes due to mortality, growth, removals, and land use; (2) mill surveys, which quantify timber volume harvested and delivered to primary wood products facilities, i.e., sawmills, pulpmills, veneer mills, composite panel mills, and pole mills; and (3) logging utilization studies, which characterize harvest operations and quantify the timber volume that is cut and utilized, as well as that portion left in the forest.

This bulletin presents the findings of a 2008 harvest and utilization study conducted in eastern Texas. The study's main goal was to provide an estimate of softwood and hardwood volume used, and of volume left in the woods as logging residue. Survey crews randomly selected and measured felled trees on 80 active harvest operations throughout the eastern Forest Inventory and Analysis (FIA) Research Work Unit regions of Texas (fig. 1). This bulletin also provides information on logging in east Texas and some general characteristics of trees harvested for various products, examples of which are average diameter at breast height (d.b.h.) by product, average bole length by product, average heights of residual stumps, and average diameter outside bark (d.o.b.) at the end of utilization.

Some standard FIA terms are used in this study. Two that are particularly important for understanding and interpreting study results are growing stock and nongrowing stock. A growing-stock tree is a live tree of commercial species that either contains or is capable of producing at least one 12-foot or two 8-foot logs in the saw-log portion of the bole. A nongrowing-stock tree is one that does not meet the requirements of growing stock due to poor form or rot. For growing-stock trees, the growing-stock portion of a tree (5-inches d.b.h. or larger) includes the volume of sound wood between a 1-foot stump and a 4-inch top, d.o.b. Volume in the 1-foot stump, volume in the main stem from 4 inches to the growing top of the tree, and the volume of any limbs 4 inches or larger with at least one 5-foot section are considered nongrowing-stock volume by FIA standards. Rough or rotten trees were also sampled and make up another piece of nongrowing stock (cull) volume. Figure 2 illustrates a poletimber and a sawtimber tree and the growing-stock section of each.

Methods

Site Stratification and Selection

Producing a complete list of timber-harvesting operations and ownerships in a region such as east Texas is problematic. Because the industry is so complex, it is impossible to list the names and locations of all during the timeframe considered in this resource bulletin. Many uncontrolled factors affect how, when, and where harvesting operations will take place; but the most common events that affect harvesting operations are weather and timber markets. A random sample provides a reasonably accurate estimate of utilization.

The sites selected for study were stratified by species group and product using the most recent data available from the Texas Forest Service publication "Harvest Trends 2007" (Xu 2008), which provides county-level output of timber products harvested in Texas by species group. Using those proportions, we designated 55 of the 80 selected sites as softwood operations, and the remaining 25 as hardwood operations. Harvest operations by product were based along these same general guidelines, although some flexibility was given to field crews for substitution due to the difficulty of locating harvesting operations for some specific products. Table 1 shows the final breakdown number of harvest operations, total trees, trees planted, and percent of trees planted by product and species group.

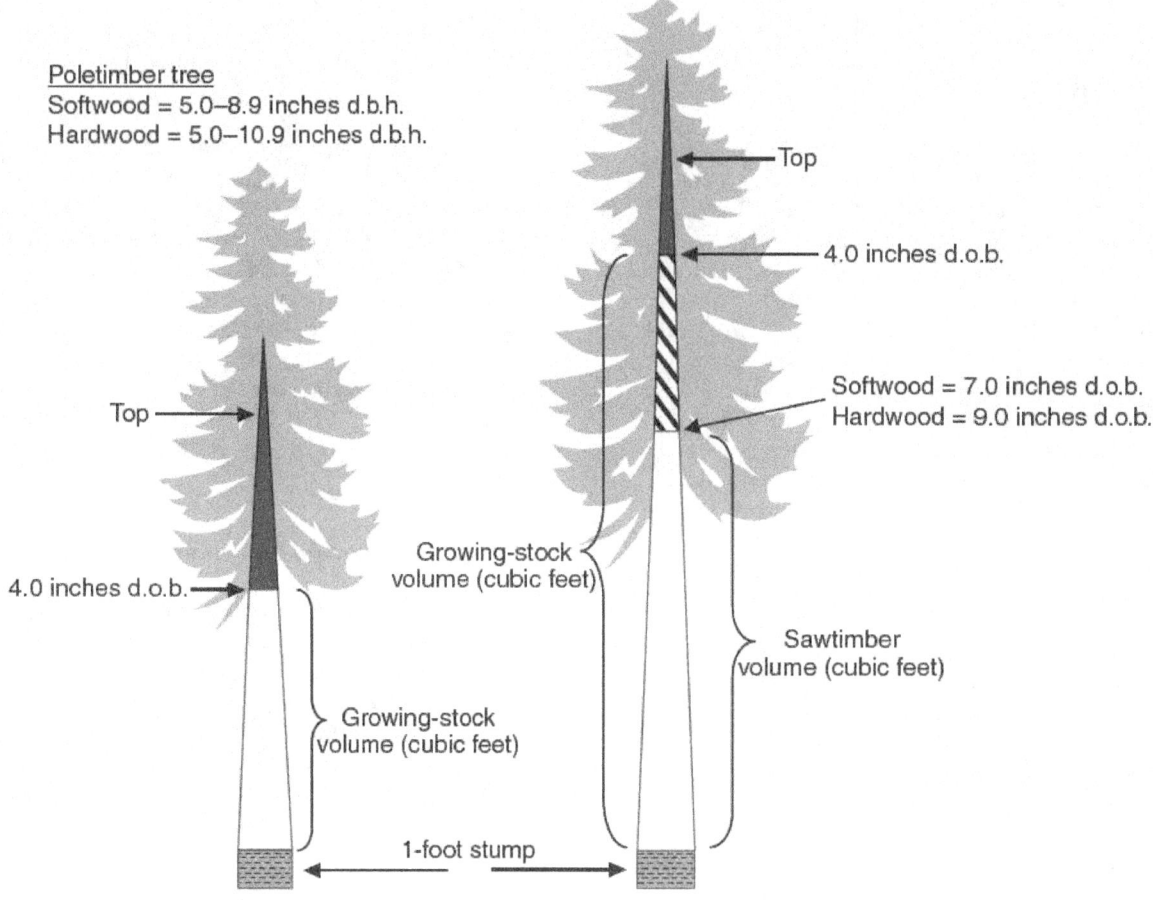

Figure 2—Stem sections of poletimber and sawtimber trees.

After the harvest operations were stratified by major species group and product, the operations were placed in the appropriate region and county in the State. Using county-level product output data from the "Harvest Trends 2007" report (Xu 2008) and a map that showed current mill locations, prospective utilization sites were selected based on a high probability of being able to locate a harvesting operation for the particular product and species group assigned. Figure 1 shows where the final harvest operations considered in this bulletin were located.

Data Collection

In May 2008, field crews were trained to collect data on felled trees at harvest locations. Using the list of operations and a map of sites, they began collecting data by county for the particular species group and designated product(s). Data were collected from May 2008 to October 2008 on active harvest operations. Field crews visited local mills and talked to county personnel to locate active harvest sites.

Table 1—Number of operations, total trees, planted trees, and percent planted by product and species group, east Texas, 2008

Product and species group	Operations	Trees Total	Planted	
		- - - - - - - - number - - - - - - - -		percent
Saw logs				
Softwood	18	463	340	73
Hardwood	10	220	0	—
Total	28	683	340	50
Veneer logs				
Softwood	17	301	98	33
Hardwood	0	0	0	—
Total	17	301	98	33
Composite panels				
Softwood	4	96	69	72
Hardwood	4	90	0	—
Total	8	186	69	37
Pulpwood				
Softwood	16	472	330	70
Hardwood	11	379	24	6
Total	27	851	354	42
Poles				
Softwood	0	3	3	100
Hardwood	0	0	0	—
Total	0	3	3	100
All products				
Softwood	55	1,335	840	63
Hardwood	25	689	24	3
Total	80	2,024	864	43

— = negligible.

At each harvest operation site, the crew members talked to the logger or the person in charge of operations. Those contacts provided vital information about product(s) utilized, specific diameters, and log lengths the receiving mill(s) would accept, along with minimum diameters at the cutoff points for specific products. Crews also noted the type of logging equipment that was being used. This information was used to determine the level of mechanization for each harvesting operation.

On each harvest operation site, the crew's goal was to measure 25 to 30 trees for each product to ensure an adequate representation of overutilization and underutilization for a given type of harvest operation. Trees were randomly selected and had to be at least 5-inches d.b.h. and alive prior to harvest. Although they often had been bucked, limbed, and topped, the main bole of each tree selected for measurement had to be intact to be measured for utilization. The State, unit, county, and location number were recorded for each site. Each tree was assigned a number and identified by species, d.b.h., tree class, product, and bole length, as well as percent cull if rot was detected. Each tree was measured from the top of the cut stump to the end of utilization. Measurements were made along the main stem in sections no longer than 16 feet until the end of utilization. The end of utilization usually is determined by the sawyer, according to particular specifications set by the receiving mill(s). Again, FIA merchantability standards for growing-stock volume are defined as the volume in the main stem of the tree from a 1-foot stump to a 4-inch top. However, most trees are not cut exactly at a 1-foot stump, nor are they cut off at exactly 4 inches. For example, trees that are cut off above a 1-foot stump and below 4 inches would be considered underutilized, and that volume not utilized would be considered growing-stock residue. On the other hand, by FIA standards, trees cut below a 1-foot stump and above a 4-inch top are considered 100 percent utilized, and those portions below and above are considered overutilization. A myriad of combinations actually occurs on active harvest operations. The aggregated volume from measured trees has provided overutilization and underutilization factors that can be applied to statewide inventory results for an estimate of growing-stock and nongrowing-stock logging residues. Other required measurements, besides d.b.h. and end of utilization, are the top of the sawtimber portion (7.0 inches in softwoods and 9.0 inches in hardwoods). Those measurements allow calculation of the sawtimber and poletimber portion of the growing-stock section.

Highlights

Characteristics of Harvested Trees in East Texas

Results of this study have identified several key characteristics of trees harvested, which cannot be obtained from a typical field inventory or a forest industry study that supplies product output data only. Characteristics such as average d.b.h. by product, average bole length by product, average residual stump height, and average d.o.b. at the end of utilization constitute important information that can help us more fully understand the complex nature of removals. Averages discussed in this section are based on the measurement of 2,024 trees. Of those, 1,335 (66 percent) were softwood, and 689 (34 percent) were hardwood.

According to the Texas "Harvest Trends 2007" report (Xu 2008), softwood and hardwood saw-log volume together accounted for 39 percent of the total product output for the State. This study classified 463 trees as having softwood saw logs averaging 12.8 inches d.b.h. Seventy-three percent, or 340 trees, were classified as planted softwood saw logs averaging 12.6 inches d.b.h. while natural softwood saw logs averaged 13.3 inches d.b.h. It classified 220 hardwood trees as having saw logs averaging 15.4 inches d.b.h. Veneer and plywood constitute another component of the product mix for east Texas. Based on 301 trees measured for softwood veneer, the average d.b.h. was 17.1 inches. Advances in lathe technology at softwood plywood mills are resulting in a drop of the average d.b.h. of peeler logs across the South. As expected, the d.b.h. of trees measured for pulpwood and composite panels was significantly smaller. Of the

472 softwood pulpwood trees measured, the average d.b.h. was 7.0 inches, while the 379 trees measured for hardwood pulpwood averaged 7.6 inches d.b.h. Seventy percent, or 330 of the softwood pulpwood trees, were planted, averaging 7.0 inches d.b.h., about the same as trees that come from natural stands. Ninety-six trees were measured for softwood composite panels and averaged 6.8 inches d.b.h., while hardwood composite panels averaged 7.7 inches d.b.h. Table 2 shows the breakdown of average d.b.h. for each product by species group and stand origin.

Bole length is the distance between a 1-foot stump and a 4-inch top. As expected, trees harvested for solid wood products tended to have longer average bole lengths than trees harvested for pulpwood or composite panel products. The average bole length for softwood trees measured for saw logs was 58 feet, while trees measured for hardwood saw logs had an average bole length of 61 feet. In comparison, trees measured for pulpwood had average bole lengths of 31 feet for both softwood and hardwood. Softwood veneer trees had an average bole length of 76 feet, while trees measured for softwood poles had an average bole length of 52 feet. Trees measured in planted stands tended to have shorter bole lengths than those measured in the natural stands. Table 3 shows the average bole length by species group, stand origin, and product.

Residual stump height is a key component in determining utilization rates for harvested trees. By FIA standards, the stump is that portion of the tree measured at ground

Table 2—Average diameter at breast height by species group, stand origin, and product, east Texas, 2008

Species group	Product				
	Saw logs	Veneer logs	Composite panels	Pulpwood	Poles
	inches				
Softwood					
Natural	13.29	17.89	6.56	7.11	—
Planted	12.55	15.59	6.83	6.98	11.93
Total	12.75	17.14	6.75	7.02	11.93
Hardwood					
Natural	15.42	—	7.67	7.58	—
Planted	—	—	—	7.98	—
Total	15.42	—	7.67	7.61	—

— = no sample for the cell.

Table 3—Average bole length by species group, stand origin, and product, east Texas, 2008

Species group and stand origin	Product				
	Saw logs	Veneer logs	Composite panels	Pulpwood	Poles
	feet				
Softwood					
Natural	60.59	78.64	24.70	32.56	—
Planted	57.06	69.46	35.70	30.29	52.33
Total	58.00	75.65	32.60	30.97	52.33
Hardwood					
Natural	60.79	—	30.91	30.19	—
Planted	—	—	—	39.63	—
Total	60.79	—	30.91	30.79	—

— = no sample for the cell.

level from the uphill side of the tree to 1 foot up the bole. Loggers try to maximize volume harvested by cutting the tree as close to the ground as possible. Residual stump heights across the products ranged from 0.33 to 0.65 feet; however, most softwood trees harvested had an average residual stump height of about a 0.40 foot, while hardwood trees harvested averaged slightly higher than one-half foot residual stumps. In softwoods and across all products, this accounted for about 43 percent of the stump volume used. In hardwoods and across all products, about 31 percent of stump volume was used. Stump volume for both hardwood and softwood contributed to utilization of the nongrowing-stock portion of trees, i.e., overutilization. Residual stump heights for trees coming from natural stands appear slightly higher than heights coming from planted stands. Table 4 shows the average residual stump heights for each product by species group.

The final component we used to determine use rates was d.o.b. at the end of utilization. Tops and limbs constitute most of the nongrowing-stock volume, although they accounted for only 32 percent of the nongrowing-stock portion that was utilized. The average end of utilization for softwood saw logs was 5.2 inches, and for hardwood saw logs 8.9 inches. The average end of utilization for softwood and hardwood pulpwood was 2.7 and 3.8 inches, respectively. Table 5 shows the average end of utilization by the different products and species group.

Table 4—Average residual stump height by species group, stand origin, and product, east Texas, 2008

Species group and stand origin	Product				
	Saw logs	Veneer logs	Composite panels	Pulpwood	Poles
	feet				
Softwood					
Natural	0.52	0.54	0.45	0.44	—
Planted	0.46	0.53	0.43	0.41	0.33
Total	0.48	0.54	0.44	0.42	0.33
Hardwood					
Natural	0.65	—	0.48	0.52	—
Planted	—	—	—	0.49	—
Total	0.65	—	0.48	0.51	—

— = no sample for the cell.

Table 5—Average end of utilization by species group, stand origin, and product, east Texas, 2008

Species group and stand origin	Product				
	Saw logs	Veneer logs	Composite panels	Pulpwood	Poles
	inches				
Softwood					
Natural	4.80	7.62	2.81	3.11	—
Planted	5.34	5.82	2.20	2.56	4.90
Total	5.19	7.03	2.37	2.72	4.90
Hardwood					
Natural	8.91	—	3.78	3.78	—
Planted	—	—	—	3.65	—
Total	8.91	—	3.78	3.78	—

— = no sample for the cell.

Softwood Removals

Results from this study document 40,431 cubic feet of softwood volume, of which 34,628 cubic feet, or 86 percent, was used for product(s). Fourteen percent, or 5,803 cubic feet, was left onsite as logging residue (fig. 3). Thirty-two percent of the residue volume came from the growing-stock portion of the tree, while 68 percent came from the nongrowing-stock portion (stumps, tops, and limbs) (fig. 4) (table A.1).

The total softwood growing-stock volume measured was 35,554 cubic feet. Of that total, 95 percent was utilized, and 5 percent was logging residue (fig. 5). By FIA merchantability standards, the logging residue portion of growing-stock trees is underutilized volume. Of the total utilized volume, 939 cubic feet, or 2.7 percent was from the nongrowing-stock portion of trees. By the same merchantability standards, that volume is considered overutilization (tables A.2 and A.3).

Softwood volumes and percentages are broken down further by poletimber and sawtimber, and by the various products measured (tables A.2 through A.7). By product, trees harvested for pulpwood and composite panels had above-average rates of utilization for the merchantable portion of the tree (98.2 and 96.3 percent, respectively) and the highest rates of overutilization (10.5 and 10.1 percent, respectively). This means that more of the nongrowing-stock portion of the tree was being used for product(s) and less was left as logging residue.

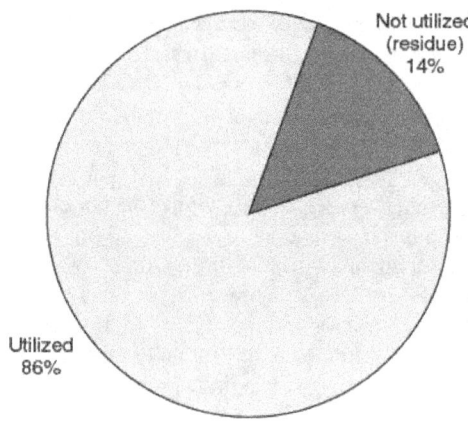

Total 40.4 thousand cubic feet

Figure 3—Disposition of total softwood harvest volume, east Texas, 2008.

Softwood percentages and volumes presented in these tables represent only trees measured in this study of 80 active harvest operations. However, it is possible to apply the percentages to inventory data from east Texas' eighth survey[1] to get an estimate of total softwood logging residues for the State. Annual softwood removal from all-live trees was 568.8 million cubic feet. Softwood growing-stock removals were 560.2 million cubic feet, or 98 percent

---

[1] Bentley, James W., Resource Forester. Texas' Forests, 2008. Manuscript in preparation. Author can be reached at U.S. Department of Agriculture Forest Service, Southern Research Station, Forest Inventory and Analysis, 4700 Old Kingston Pike, Knoxville, TN 37919.

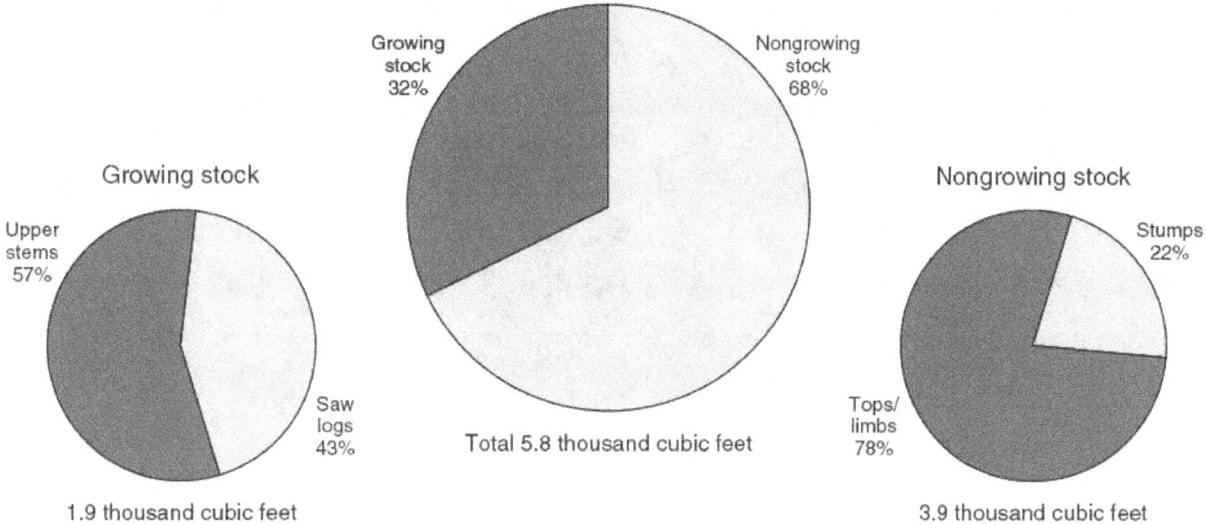

Figure 4—Softwood residue by volume type, east Texas, 2008.

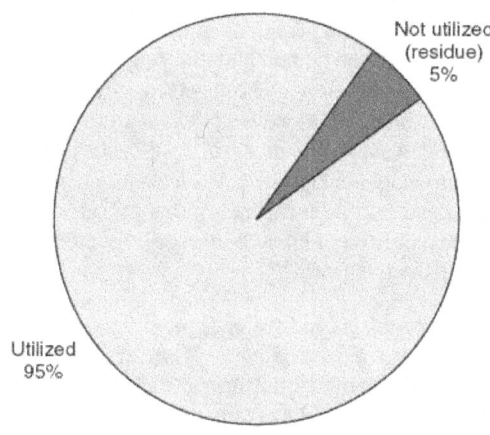

Total 35.6 thousand cubic feet

Figure 5—Disposition of softwood growing-stock volume, east Texas, 2008.

of the total. Applying the factors from this study to total softwood removals for all-live trees tallied in the east Texas survey provides an estimate of 124.0 million cubic feet total annual softwood residue. Of the total residue for all-live trees, 37.0 million cubic feet, or 30 percent, was considered growing-stock residue. The remaining 70 percent, or 86.9 million cubic feet, was nongrowing-stock residue from stumps, tops, and limbs, as well as cull trees not used.

Hardwood Removals

Results from this study document 15,094 cubic feet of hardwood volume, of which 11,252 cubic feet, or 75 percent, was utilized for product(s). Twenty-five percent, or 3,842 cubic feet, was left onsite as logging residue (fig. 6). Thirty-five percent of residue volume came from the growing-stock portion of trees, and 65 percent came from the nongrowing-stock portion (stumps, tops, and limbs) (fig. 7) (table A.1).

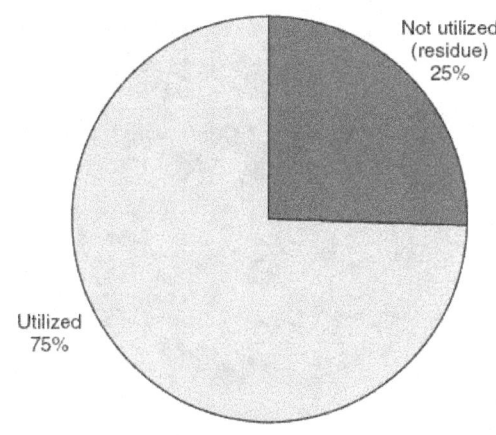

Total 15.1 thousand cubic feet

Figure 6—Disposition of total hardwood harvest volume, east Texas, 2008.

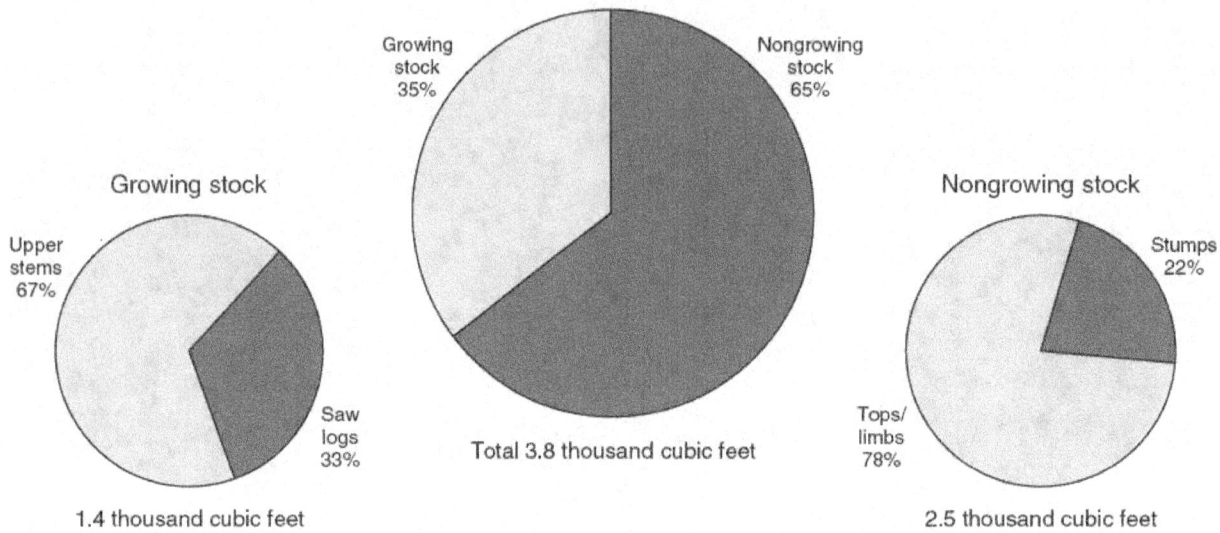

Figure 7—Hardwood residue by volume type, east Texas, 2008.

The total hardwood growing-stock volume measured was 12,240 cubic feet. Of that total, 89 percent was used, and 11 percent was logging residue (fig. 8). By FIA merchantability standards, the logging residue portion is underutilized volume. Of the total utilized volume, 370 cubic feet, or 3.3 percent, was from the nongrowing-stock portion of trees. By the same merchantability standards, that volume is considered overutilization (tables A.8 and A.9).

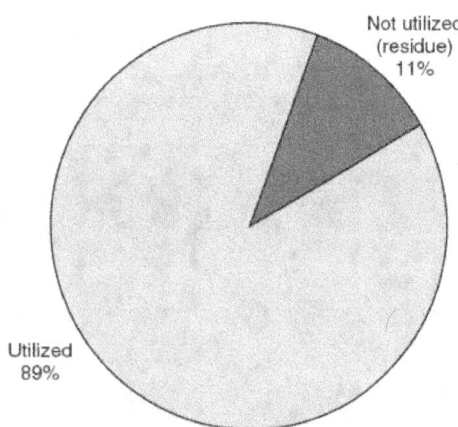

Figure 8—Disposition of hardwood growing-stock volume, east Texas, 2008.

Hardwood volumes and percentages also were measured for poletimber and sawtimber, and differentiated by the various products they provided (tables A.8 through A.15). At 93 percent, however, those trees measured for pulpwood and composite panels were more fully utilized. Also, more of the nongrowing-stock portion was used for pulpwood and composite panels. Trees measured for hardwood saw logs were the least utilized of all, although they have the most nongrowing-stock material.

Hardwood percentages and volumes presented in the tables represent just trees measured in this study of 80 active harvest operations. However, it is possible to apply the percentages to inventory data from east Texas' eighth survey (see footnote 1 on page 6) to provide an estimate of total hardwood logging residue for the State. Annual hardwood removals from all-live trees totaled 189.5 million cubic feet. Hardwood growing-stock removals totaled 161.1 million cubic feet, or 85 percent of that total. Applying factors from this study to total hardwood removals from all-live trees tallied in the east Texas survey provided an estimate of 48.8 million cubic feet total annual hardwood residue. Of that total, 22.9 million cubic feet, or 47 percent, was considered growing-stock residue. The remaining 53 percent, or 25.8 million cubic feet, was nongrowing-stock residue from stumps, tops, and limbs, and rough or rotten trees that were not used.

East Texas Potential Biomass Availability

Logging residue has long been viewed as a possible source for bioenergy and other timber products, although traditionally it has not had any merchantable value. Retrieval of logging residue is a matter of economics, based on markets or demand. If markets for wood products are available and a willingness to pay a reasonable price exists, then more total tree volume is utilized for products. With this in mind, logging residue volume for the period 2004 to 2008, or eighth survey, in east Texas amounted to 172.7 million cubic feet, or 6.2 million green tons. Nearly 124 million cubic feet (4.3 million tons), or 72 percent, of the logging residues generated came from softwoods, while 48.8 million cubic feet (1.9 million tons) came from hardwood species. Logging residue from the merchantable portion of all-live tree removals totaled 64.9 million cubic feet (2.4 million tons), or nearly 38 percent of the total logging residue. Other sources accounted for 107.9 million cubic feet (3.8 million tons), or 62 percent of the total logging residue. Trees <5 inches d.b.h contributed another 2.4 million tons of possible logging residue. Tables 6 and 7 express the volume of timber removals by removals class, species group, and source in million cubic feet and green tons.

Over the same time period, the area of timber harvested annually in east Texas amounted to 545,500 acres. Of this area, 174,400 acres (32 percent) underwent a final harvest, while 136,800 acres (25 percent) had a partial harvest and 219,400 acres (40 percent) had commercial thinning. The removals volume attributed to timber products and logging residues are directly related to these treated acres. Based on these estimates, we can say that 54.8 tons per acre in the merchantable and nonmerchantable portion of trees >5 inches d.b.h. were removed annually from east Texas timberland. Of this, 43.5 tons per acre were utilized for products, while 10.1 tons per acre were left as logging residue, excluding the residual stump. Assuming a 20-percent recovery rate for trees <5 inches d.b.h., an additional 0.9 tons per acre was added bringing the total logging residue to 11.0 tons per acre. This volume of

Table 6—Volume of timber removals by removals class, species group, and source, east Texas, 2008

Removals class and species group	All sources	Source	
		All-live removals	Other sources
	million cubic feet		
Roundwood products			
Softwood	533.3	497.4	35.9
Hardwood	137.4	120.5	16.9
Total	670.7	617.8	52.8
Logging residues			
Softwood	124.0	37.6	86.3
Hardwood	48.8	27.2	21.5
Total	172.7	64.9	107.9
Other removals			
Softwood	41.6	33.8	7.7
Hardwood	52.7	41.8	10.9
Total	94.3	75.7	18.6
Total removals			
Softwood	698.8	568.8	130.0
Hardwood	238.8	189.5	49.3
Total	937.6	758.3	179.3

Numbers in rows and columns may not sum to totals due to rounding.

Table 7—Volume of timber removals by removals class, species group, and source, east Texas, 2008

Removals class and species group	All sources	Source	
		All-live removals	Other sources
		green tons	
Roundwood products			
Softwood	18,398,526	17,158,891	1,239,635
Hardwood	5,313,899	4,659,516	654,383
Total	23,712,425	21,818,407	1,894,018
Logging residues			
Softwood	4,276,702	1,297,665	2,979,037
Hardwood	1,885,869	1,053,697	832,172
Total	6,162,571	2,351,362	3,811,209
Other removals			
Softwood	1,433,631	1,166,977	266,654
Hardwood	2,039,043	1,617,990	421,053
Total	3,472,674	2,784,967	687,707
Total removals			
Softwood	24,108,859	19,623,533	4,485,326
Hardwood	9,238,811	7,331,203	1,907,608
Total	33,347,670	26,954,736	6,392,934

logging residue would be the equivalent of about one-half of a tree-length trailer load of wood for every acre treated in east Texas.

Most loggers are very well equipped to handle the main bole or merchantable portion of the tree and even long straight sections of forks or major limbs. However, a more effective way to handle rough trees with crooked boles, tops, and limbs is to chip this material at the site and transport the material in chip vans. Whole trees and portions of trees chipped onsite have a very limited use for industrial timber products. Mulch or boiler fuel are about the only uses for this kind of material. Where bioenergy or mulch markets are available, this is a particularly cost efficient way of dealing with small trees < 5 inches d.b.h., and rough and rotten trees, as well as the nonmerchantable portions of growing-stock trees. Current literature suggests that, with conventional logging equipment, a 60-percent recovery rate is a realistic goal for possible extraction of formerly unutilized material (Perlack and others 2005). At this recovery rate, an additional 6.6 tons per acre of material once classified as logging residue could be added to the volume going for timber products.

Literature Cited

Bechtold, W.A.; Patterson, P.L., eds. 2005.The enhanced forest inventory and analysis program–national sampling design and estimation procedures. Gen. Tech. Rep. SRS–80. Asheville, NC: U.S. Department of Agriculture Forest Service, Southern Research Station. 85 p.

Perlack, R.D.; Wright, L.L.; Turhollow, A. [and others]. 2005. Biomass as feedstock for a bioenergy and bioproducts industry: the technical feasibility of a billion-ton annual supply. ORNL/TM-2005/66. Washington, DC: U.S. Department of Energy and U.S. Department of Agriculture Forest Service. 73 p.

Xu, W. 2008. Texas timber harvest trends 2007. 21 p. http://txforestservice.tamu.edu/uploadedFiles/Sustainable/econdev/2007%20 Harvest%20 Trends%20.pdf. [Date accessed: March 5, 2009].

Glossary

Board foot. Unit of measure applied to roundwood. It relates to lumber that is 1-foot long, 1-foot wide, and 1-inch thick (or its equivalent).

Composite products. Roundwood products manufactured into chips, wafers, strands, flakes, shavings, or sawdust and then reconstituted into a variety of panel and engineered lumber products.

Drain. The volume of roundwood removed from any geographic area where timber is grown.

Growing-stock removals. The growing-stock volume removed from poletimber and sawtimber trees in the timberland inventory. (Note: Includes volume removed for roundwood products, logging residues, and other removals.)

Growing-stock trees. Living trees of commercial species classified as sawtimber, poletimber, saplings, and seedlings. Growing-stock trees must contain at least one 12-foot or two 8-foot logs in the saw-log portion, currently or potentially (if too small to qualify). The log(s) must meet dimension and merchantability standards and have, currently or potentially, one-third of the gross board-foot volume in sound wood.

Growing-stock volume. The cubic-foot volume of sound wood in growing-stock trees at least 5.0 inches d.b.h. from a 1-foot stump to a minimum 4.0-inch top d.o.b. of the central stem.

Hardwoods. Dicotyledonous trees, usually broadleaf and deciduous.

   Soft hardwoods. Hardwood species with an average specific gravity of 0.50 or less, such as gums, yellow-poplar, cottonwoods, red maple, basswoods, and willows.

   Hard hardwoods. Hardwood species with an average specific gravity > 0.50, such as oaks, hard maples, hickories, and beech.

Industrial roundwood products. Any primary use of the main stem of a tree, such as saw logs, pulpwood, and veneer logs, intended to be processed into primary wood products, such as lumber, wood pulp, and sheathing, at primary wood-using mills.

International ¼-inch rule. A log rule or formula for estimating the board-foot volume of logs, allowing ½-inch of taper for each 4-foot length. The rule appears in a number of forms that allow for kerf. In the form used by FIA, a ¼-inch of kerf is assumed. This rule is used as the USDA Forest Service standard log rule in the Eastern United States.

Log. A primary forest product harvested in long, primarily 8-, 12-, and 16-foot lengths.

Logging residues. The unused merchantable portion of growing-stock trees cut or destroyed during logging operations.

Merchantable portion. That portion of live trees 5.0 inches d.b.h. and larger between a 1-foot stump and a minimum 4.0-inch top d.o.b. on the central stem. That portion of primary forks from the point of occurrence to a minimum 4.0-inch top d.o.b. is included.

Merchantable volume. Solid-wood volume in the merchantable portion of live trees.

Noncommercial species. Tree species of typically small size, poor form, or inferior quality that normally do not develop into trees suitable for industrial wood products.

Nonforest land. Land that has never supported forests and land formerly forested where timber production is precluded by development for other uses.

Nongrowing-stock sources. The net volume removed from the nongrowing-stock portions of poletimber and sawtimber trees (stumps, tops, limbs, cull sections of central stem) and from any portion of a rough, rotten, sapling, dead, or nonforest tree.

Other forest land. Forest land other than timberland and productive reserved forest land. It includes available and reserved forest land that is incapable of producing annually 20 cubic feet per acre of industrial wood under natural conditions because of adverse site conditions such as sterile soils, dry climate, poor drainage, high elevation, steepness, or rockiness.

Other products. A miscellaneous category of roundwood products, e.g., cooperage, excelsior, shingles, and mill residue byproducts (charcoal, bedding, mulch, etc.).

Other removals. The growing-stock volume of trees removed from the inventory by cultural operations such as timber stand improvement, land clearing, and other changes in land use, resulting in the removal of the trees from timberland.

Other sources. (See: Nongrowing-stock sources.)

Poletimber-size trees. Softwoods 5.0 to 8.9 inches d.b.h. and hardwoods 5.0 to 10.9 inches d.b.h.

Posts, poles, and pilings. Roundwood products milled (cut or peeled) into standard sizes (lengths and circumferences) to be put in the ground to provide vertical and lateral support in buildings, foundations, utility lines, and fences. May also include nonindustrial (unmilled) products.

Primary wood-using plants. Industries that convert roundwood products (saw logs, veneer logs, pulpwood, etc.) into primary wood products, such as lumber, veneer or sheathing, and wood pulp.

Pulpwood. A roundwood product that will be reduced to individual wood fibers by chemical or mechanical means. The fibers are used to make a broad generic group of pulp products that includes paper products, as well as chipboard, fiberboard, insulating board, and paperboard.

Rotten trees. Live trees of commercial species not containing at least one 12-foot saw log, or two noncontiguous saw logs, each 8 feet or longer, now or prospectively, primarily because of rot or missing sections, and with less than one-third of the gross board-foot tree volume in sound material.

Rough trees. Live trees of commercial species not containing at least one 12-foot saw log, or two noncontiguous saw logs, each 8 feet or longer, now or prospectively, primarily because of roughness, poor form, splits, and cracks, and with less than one-third of the gross board-foot tree volume in sound material; and live trees of noncommercial species.

Roundwood (roundwood logs). Logs, bolts, or other round sections cut from trees for industrial manufacture or consumer uses.

Roundwood chipped. Any timber cut primarily for industrial manufacture, delivered to nonpulpmills, chipped, and then sold to pulpmills for use as fiber. Includes tops, jump sections, whole trees, and pulpwood sticks.

Roundwood product drain. That portion of total drain used for a product.

Roundwood products. Any primary product, such as lumber, poles, pilings, pulp, or fuelwood that is produced from roundwood.

Salvable dead trees. Standing or downed dead trees that were formerly growing stock and considered merchantable. Trees must be at least 5.0 inches d.b.h. to qualify.

Saplings. Live trees 1.0 to 5.0 inches d.b.h.

Saw log. A roundwood product, usually 8 feet in length or longer, processed into a variety of sawn products such as lumber, cants, pallets, railroad ties, and timbers.

Saw-log portion. The part of the bole of sawtimber trees between a 1-foot stump and the saw-log top.

Saw-log top. The point on the bole of sawtimber trees above which a conventional saw log cannot be produced. The minimum saw-log top is 7.0 inches d.o.b. for softwoods and 9.0 inches d.o.b. for hardwoods.

Sawtimber-size trees. Softwoods 9.0 inches d.b.h. and larger and hardwoods 11.0 inches d.b.h. and larger.

Sawtimber volume. Growing-stock volume in the saw-log portion of sawtimber-sized trees in board feet (International ¼-inch rule).

Seedlings. Trees < 1.0 inch d.b.h. and > 1 foot tall for hardwoods, > 6 inches tall for softwood, and > 0.5 inch in diameter at ground level for longleaf pine.

Softwoods. Coniferous trees, usually evergreen, having leaves that are needles or scalelike.

Standard cord. A unit of measure applied to roundwood, usually bolts or split wood. It is a stack of wood 4 feet high, 4 feet wide, and 8 feet long encompassing 128 cubic feet of wood, bark, and air space. This usually translates to approximately 75.0 to 81.0 cubic feet of solid wood for pulpwood, because pulpwood is more uniform.

Standard unit. A unit measure applied to roundwood timber products. Board feet (International ¼-inch rule) is the standard unit used for saw logs and veneer; cords are used for pulpwood, composite panel, and fuelwood; hundred pieces for poles; thousand pieces for posts; and thousand cubic feet for all other miscellaneous forest products.

Timberland. Forest land capable of producing 20 cubic feet of industrial wood per acre per year and not withdrawn from timber utilization.

Timber product output. The total volume of roundwood products from all sources plus the volume of byproducts recovered from mill residues (equals roundwood product drain).

Timber products. Roundwood products and byproducts.

Timber removals. The total volume of trees removed from the timberland inventory by harvesting, cultural operations such as stand improvement, land clearing, or changes in land use. (Note: Includes roundwood products, logging residues, and other removals.)

Tree. Woody plant having one erect perennial stem or trunk at least 3 inches d.b.h., a more or less definitely formed crown of foliage, and a height of at least 13 feet (at maturity).

Upper-stem portion. The part of the main stem of sawtimber trees above the saw-log top and the minimum top diameter of 4.0 inches outside bark, or to the point where the main stem breaks into limbs.

Utilization studies. Studies conducted on active logging operations to develop factors for merchantable portions of trees left in the woods (logging residues), logging damage, and utilization of the unmerchantable portion of growing-stock trees and nongrowing-stock trees.

Veneer log. A roundwood product either rotary cut, sliced, stamped, or sawn into a variety of veneer products such as plywood, finished panels, veneer sheets, or sheathing.

Weight. A unit of measure for mill residues, expressed as oven-dry tons (2,000 oven-dry pounds).

Appendix

Index of Tables

Table A.1—Harvest and utilization volume by species group, source, and volume type, east Texas, 2008

Species group and source	Total tree volume	Growing stock					Nongrowing stock				
		Total	Saw log		Upper stem		Total	Stumps		Tops/limbs	
			Utilized	Not utilized	Utilized	Not utilized		Utilized	Not utilized	Utilized	Not utilized
					cubic feet						
Softwood											
Sawtimber	37,204.30	32,946.33	30,219.04	810.21	876.27	1,040.81	4,257.97	554.72	761.01	37.58	2,904.66
Poletimber	3,226.40	2,607.67	—	—	2,592.95	14.72	618.73	96.01	91.44	250.96	180.32
Total	40,430.70	35,554.00	30,219.04	810.21	3,469.22	1,055.53	4,876.70	650.73	852.45	288.54	3,084.98
Hardwood											
Sawtimber	11,856.78	9,693.07	7,952.04	442.47	517.81	780.75	2,163.71	143.90	414.77	11.33	1,593.71
Poletimber	3,237.32	2,546.96	—	—	2,411.58	135.38	690.36	98.41	125.78	116.54	349.63
Total	15,094.10	12,240.03	7,952.04	442.47	2,929.39	916.13	2,854.07	242.31	540.55	127.87	1,943.34

— = no sample for the cell.

Table A.2—Volume of softwood growing stock by product and utilization for sawtimber and poletimber, east Texas, 2008

Product	Total volume utilized	Growing stock			Nongrowing stock utilized	Saw-log portion			
		Total	Utilized	Not utilized		Total	Utilized	Cull utilized	Not utilized
					cubic feet				
Saw logs	12,906.99	13,321.45	12,612.08	709.37	294.91	12,189.94	11,795.86	284.10	109.98
Veneer logs	18,144.05	18,950.01	17,866.88	1,083.13	277.17	18,084.42	17,701.44	-30.93	413.91
Composite panels	675.55	630.26	607.02	23.24	68.53	187.09	175.16	11.69	0.24
Pulpwood	2,835.22	2,586.56	2,538.73	47.83	296.49	507.03	485.80	21.23	—
Poles	65.72	65.71	63.55	2.16	2.17	60.79	60.79	—	—
Total	34,627.53	35,554.00	33,688.26	1,865.73	939.27	31,029.27	30,219.05	286.09	524.13

Numbers in rows and columns may not sum to totals due to rounding.
— = no sample for the cell.

Table A.3—Percent of overutilization and underutilization for softwood growing stock by product for sawtimber and poletimber, east Texas, 2008

Product	Overutilization		Underutilization		Saw-log portion		
	Growing stock utilized/ total volume utilized	Nongrowing stock utilized/ total volume utilized	Growing stock utilized/total growing-stock volume	Growing stock not utilized/ total growing-stock volume	Saw log utilized/ total saw-log volume	Cull utilized/ total saw-log volume	Saw log not utilized/ total saw-log volume
				percent			
Saw logs	97.72	2.28	94.67	5.33	96.77	2.33	0.90
Veneer logs	98.47	1.53	94.28	5.72	97.88	-0.17	2.29
Composite panels	89.86	10.14	96.31	3.69	93.62	6.25	0.13
Pulpwood	89.54	10.46	98.15	1.85	95.81	4.19	—
Poles	96.70	3.30	96.71	3.29	100.00	—	—
All products	97.29	2.71	94.75	5.25	97.39	0.92	1.69

— = no sample for the cell.

Table A.4—Volume of softwood growing stock by product and utilization for sawtimber, east Texas, 2008

Product	Total volume utilized	Growing stock			Nongrowing stock utilized	Saw-log portion			
		Total	Utilized	Not utilized		Total	Utilized	Cull utilized	Not utilized
					cubic feet				
Saw logs	12,642.80	13,061.28	12,358.87	702.41	283.93	12,189.94	11,795.86	284.10	109.98
Veneer logs	18,144.05	18,950.01	17,866.88	1,083.13	277.17	18,084.42	17,701.44	-30.93	413.91
Composite panels	191.81	211.09	188.48	22.61	3.33	187.09	175.16	11.69	0.24
Pulpwood	643.24	658.25	617.54	40.71	25.70	507.03	485.80	21.23	—
Poles	65.72	65.71	63.55	2.16	2.17	60.79	60.79	—	—
Total	31,687.62	32,946.33	31,095.32	1,851.02	592.30	31,029.27	30,219.05	286.09	524.13

Numbers in rows and columns may not sum to totals due to rounding.
— = no sample for the cell.

Table A.5—Percent of overutilization and underutilization for softwood growing stock by product for sawtimber, east Texas, 2008

Product	Overutilization		Underutilization		Saw-log portion		
	Growing stock utilized/ total volume utilized	Nongrowing stock utilized/ total volume utilized	Growing stock utilized/total growing-stock volume	Growing stock not utilized/ total growing-stock volume	Saw log utilized/ total saw-log volume	Cull utilized/ total saw-log volume	Saw log not utilized/ total saw-log volume
	percent						
Saw logs	97.75	2.25	94.62	5.38	96.77	2.33	0.90
Veneer logs	98.47	1.53	94.28	5.72	97.88	-0.17	2.29
Composite panels	98.26	1.74	89.29	10.71	93.62	6.25	0.13
Pulpwood	96.00	4.00	93.82	6.18	95.81	4.19	—
Poles	96.70	3.30	96.71	3.29	100.00	—	—
All products	98.13	1.87	94.38	5.62	97.39	0.92	1.69

— = no sample for the cell.

Table A.6—Volume of softwood growing stock by product and utilization for poletimber, east Texas, 2008

Product	Total volume utilized	Growing stock			Nongrowing stock utilized
		Total	Utilized	Not utilized	
	cubic feet				
Saw logs	264.19	260.17	253.21	6.96	10.98
Veneer logs	—	—	—	—	—
Composite panels	483.74	419.17	418.54	0.63	65.20
Pulpwood	2,191.98	1,928.31	1,921.19	7.12	270.79
Poles	—	—	—	—	—
Total	2,939.91	2,607.65	2,592.94	14.71	346.97

Numbers in rows and columns may not sum to totals due to rounding.

— = no sample for the cell.

Table A.7—Percent of overutilization and underutilization for softwood growing stock by product for poletimber, east Texas, 2008

	Overutilization		Underutilization	
Product	Growing stock utilized/ total volume utilized	Nongrowing stock utilized/ total volume utilized	Growing stock utilized/total growing-stock volume	Growing stock not utilized/ total growing-stock volume
	percent			
Saw logs	95.84	4.16	97.32	2.68
Veneer logs	—	—	—	—
Composite panels	86.52	13.48	99.85	0.15
Pulpwood	87.65	12.35	99.63	0.37
Poles	—	—	—	—
All products	88.20	11.80	99.44	0.56

— = no sample for the cell.

Table A.8—Volume of hardwood growing stock by product and utilization for sawtimber and poletimber, east Texas, 2008

		Growing stock				Saw-log portion			
Product	Total volume utilized	Total	Utilized	Not utilized	Nongrowing stock utilized	Total	Utilized	Cull utilized	Not utilized
	cubic feet								
Saw logs	8,046.08	9,030.50	7,905.02	1,125.48	141.06	7,818.52	7,438.29	-35.08	415.31
Veneer logs	—	—	—	—	—	—	—	—	—
Composite panels	581.35	581.73	538.66	43.07	42.69	83.44	68.52	14.92	—
Pulpwood	2,624.19	2,627.80	2,437.76	190.04	186.43	492.55	445.22	34.98	12.34
Poles	—	—	—	—	—	—	—	—	—
Total	11,251.62	12,240.03	10,881.44	1,358.59	370.18	8,394.51	7,952.03	14.82	427.65

Numbers in rows and columns may not sum to totals due to rounding.
— = no sample for the cell.

Table A.9—Percent of overutilization and underutilization for hardwood growing stock by product for sawtimber and poletimber, east Texas, 2008

Product	Overutilization		Underutilization		Saw-log portion		
	Growing stock utilized/ total volume utilized	Nongrowing stock utilized/ total volume utilized	Growing stock utilized/total growing-stock volume	Growing stock not utilized/ total growing-stock volume	Saw log utilized/ total saw-log volume	Cull utilized/ total saw-log volume	Saw log not utilized/ total saw-log volume
	percent						
Saw logs	98.25	1.75	87.54	12.46	95.14	-0.45	5.31
Veneer logs	—	—	—	—	—	—	—
Composite panels	92.66	7.34	92.60	7.41	82.12	17.88	—
Pulpwood	92.90	7.10	92.77	7.23	90.39	7.10	2.51
Poles	—	—	—	—	—	—	—
All products	96.71	3.29	88.90	11.10	94.73	0.18	5.09

— = no sample for the cell.

Table A.10—Volume of hardwood growing stock by product and utilization for sawtimber, east Texas, 2008

Product	Total volume utilized	Growing stock			Nongrowing stock utilized	Saw-log portion			
		Total	Utilized	Not utilized		Total	Utilized	Cull utilized	Not utilized
		cubic feet							
Saw logs	7,983.16	8,963.43	7,845.43	1,118.00	137.73	7,818.52	7,438.29	-35.08	415.31
Veneer logs	—	—	—	—	—	—	—	—	—
Composite panels	90.06	109.23	86.92	22.31	3.14	83.44	68.52	14.92	—
Pulpwood	551.87	620.42	537.51	82.91	14.36	492.55	445.22	34.98	12.34
Poles	—	—	—	—	—	—	—	—	—
Total	8,625.09	9,693.08	8,469.86	1,223.22	155.23	8,394.51	7,952.03	14.82	427.65

Numbers in rows and columns may not sum to totals due to rounding.

— = no sample for the cell.

Table A.11—Percent of overutilization and underutilization for hardwood growing stock by product for sawtimber, east Texas, 2008

Product	Overutilization		Underutilization		Saw-log portion		
	Growing stock utilized/ total volume utilized	Nongrowing stock utilized/ total volume utilized	Growing stock utilized/total growing-stock volume	Growing stock not utilized/ total growing-stock volume	Saw log utilized/ total saw-log volume	Cull utilized/ total saw-log volume	Saw log not utilized/ total saw-log volume
				percent			
Saw logs	98.27	1.73	87.53	12.47	95.14	-0.45	5.31
Veneer logs	—	—	—	—	—	—	—
Composite panels	96.51	3.49	79.58	20.42	82.12	17.88	—
Pulpwood	97.40	2.60	86.64	13.36	90.39	7.10	2.51
Poles	—	—	—	—	—	—	—
All products	98.20	1.80	87.38	12.62	94.73	0.18	5.09

— = no sample for the cell.

Table A.12—Volume of hardwood growing stock by product and utilization for poletimber, east Texas, 2008

Product	Total volume utilized	Growing stock			Nongrowing stock utilized
		Total	Utilized	Not utilized	
			cubic feet		
Saw logs	62.92	67.07	59.59	7.48	3.33
Veneer logs	—	—	—	—	—
Composite panels	491.29	472.50	451.74	20.76	39.55
Pulpwood	2,072.32	2,007.38	1,900.25	107.13	172.07
Poles	—	—	—	—	—
Total	2,626.53	2,546.95	2,411.58	135.37	214.95

Numbers in rows and columns may not sum to totals due to rounding.

— = no sample for the cell.

Table A.13—Percent of overutilization and underutilization for hardwood growing stock by product for poletimber, east Texas, 2008

Product	Overutilization		Underutilization	
	Growing stock utilized/ total volume utilized	Nongrowing stock utilized/ total volume utilized	Growing stock utilized/total growing-stock volume	Growing stock not utilized/ total growing-stock volume
	percent			
Saw logs	94.71	5.29	88.85	11.15
Veneer logs	—	—	—	—
Composite panels	91.95	8.05	95.61	4.39
Pulpwood	91.70	8.30	94.66	5.34
Poles	—	—	—	—
All products	91.82	8.18	94.69	5.31

— = no sample for the cell.

Table A.14—Volume of hardwood cull by product and utilization, east Texas, 2008

Product	Total volume utilized	Nongrowing stock			
		Merchantable			
		Total	Utilized	Not utilized	Unmerchantable utilized
		cubic feet			
Saw logs	—	—	—	—	—
Veneer logs	—	—	—	—	—
Composite panels	13.65	13.43	13.20	0.23	0.45
Pulpwood	19.12	16.48	15.83	0.65	3.29
Poles	—	—	—	—	—
Total	32.77	29.91	29.03	0.88	3.74

Numbers in rows and columns may not sum to totals due to rounding.

— = no sample for the cell.

Table A.15—Percent of overutilization and underutilization for hardwood cull by product, east Texas, 2008

Product	Overutilization		Underutilization	
	Merchantable utilized/ total volume utilized	Unmerchantable utilized/ total volume utilized	Merchantable utilized/total merchantable volume	Merchantable not utilized/ total merchantable volume
	percent			
Saw logs	—	—	—	—
Veneer logs	—	—	—	—
Composite panels	96.70	3.30	98.29	1.71
Pulpwood	82.79	17.21	96.06	3.94
Poles	—	—	—	—
All products	88.59	11.41	97.06	2.94

— = no sample for the cell.